A DOG'S Guide to CATS

KAREN DAVISON

With Bob the Westie

Published by SmartDog Books, Ireland
Copyright Karen Davison 2016
All rights reserved

ISBN-13: 978-1539503040
ISBN-10: 1539503046

TABLE OF CONTENTS

INTRODUCTION

Before we begin, I wish to thank all my canine friends for the fan mail.

I'm glad that so many of you found *A Dog's Guide to Humans* helpful. Some of you achieved remarkable success in training humans to do all sorts of weird and wonderful things, so keep up the good work!

Now, by popular demand I have once again put paw to paper to offer a few pearls of wisdom about a far more challenging species, the old enemy… Cats.

In these pages I will share some of the emails and letters that have poured in, some heart wrenching and cautionary tales of how cats make life miserable for our trusting, and some would say more naive species.

Roxi the Lab has also given kind permission for me to share her blog post 'Cats vs Dogs -Inequality in The Den', an interesting article that I think most of us will relate to.

Roxi puts forward a radical proposal for a permanent solution to the cat problem which is certainly food for thought.

Even if you're lucky enough not to share your den with one of the beasts, cats are EVERYWHERE. I tell you my friends, no matter how much pee you spray around your boundary, they just ignore it... their arrogance knows no bounds.

Cats are unavoidable, so you will probably have to deal with one sooner or later. Don't be fooled by their apparent small stature and fluffy cuteness, these things have superpowers that you can only dream of (more about this later), and their instincts are as sharp as their claws.

Luckily help is at hand. *A Dog's Guide to Cats* contains all you need to get one step ahead of the game.

This book explains the feline weapon system, cat ambush techniques and how to avoid them, cat safety tips and how to act to maintain the myth that we dogs are 'well able' for cats.

As an added bonus, I will also share with you some vital information! I have discovered that our enemy has an Achilles Heel. Yes my friends, cats have a weakness... Who knew?

After many years of extensive scientific research

and much trial and error, I have taken advantage of this flaw to design a system to lure cats into a cunning trap that will give you hours of guaranteed cat-free pleasure.

> We stand united.
> Woof, woof,
> Bob the Westie.

LETTER FROM SIR CECIL
OF INDIGO MOON (AKA DIESEL)

Dear Bob,

Do we get punished for being naughty in a former life?

The reason I ask is I can't think of anything that I've done in this one, that would result in me being forced to share my den with fourteen cats.

I'm a good boy, or so I'm told, so why is this happening to me?

I can't get any peace, I'm stalked every-where I go.

I daren't sleep, and when I do fall into an exhausted doze, terrible images haunt my dreams.

Last week, I managed to dismantle the fence and break out. I had a taste of freedom, but it wasn't quite what I expected. They are out there as well, in the trees, lurking under cars, hiding in the bushes...

... Luckily the dog warden grabbed me and took me to the pound. In that cold kennel, there were no cats at all!

Finally! I got the best night's sleep I'd had in ages. Sadly my elation was short lived, my pesky microchip gave me away and I was sent back to the den of continued suffering. I dream of getting a small kennel by the sea. (I heard cat's don't like water) But I need cash.

I've started a GoFundMe campaign: Sir Cecil's End of Rope Escape Fund. Any donations would be gratefully received.

Yours hopefully,

Sir Cecil
(AKA Diesel)

BOB'S REPLY TO SIR CECIL

Bob the Westie,
Painswick,
The Cotswolds,
Gloucestershire.

Dear Diesel,

I hope you don't mind my informal address, I feel like we are friends already!

I can't imagine how distressing it is for you being subjected to such horrendous conditions, but rest assured, the situation you find yourself in has nothing to do with karma and more to do with poor home choices. We all make mistakes.

It pains me to hear of a fellow canine having such a hard time and I promise to do everything in my power to help you. I have already organised a whip round, the response from our comrades has been incredible. I have forwarded the funds collected so far to your GoFundMe campaign.

One of my good friends, Bilbo Baggins, is in the process of organising a sponsored human walk to raise further cash for your appeal. The support so far has been fantastic. We aim to get you out of there ASAP.

Sending love and support,
Woof, woof,
Bob

*** Will Sir Cecil get the funds for his great escape?
Find out later.**

CHOOSING YOUR COMPANION

Sadly for Sir Cecil, this advice comes too late. But for those of you who have not yet chosen a home, it's possible to minimise the risks of being lumbered with cats by giving careful consideration to which subspecies of human you choose. Careful selection at this stage can save you a whole pile of stress later on.

Here is a quick run down on the different breeds.

DOG LOVERS

The best type of human to share your den with! Dog lovers tend to be sociable, affectionate, fun to hang out with and an ideal choice to spend your life with.

They enjoy having cuddles, playing with toys and being taken for long and interesting walks.

Good company, great fun and usually moderately easy to train, you couldn't ask for more in a companion.

CRAZY CAT PERSON

Crazy cat people are obsessed with cats and often collect a large number of them. Just what they get out of this arrangement is a bit of a mystery.

Little is known about this subspecies of human. I can only surmise that their characters must be a good match for their preferred pets. Unsociable, lazy and aggressive if challenged.

Luckily for us, their poor taste in companionship means that we're safe. (Providing they don't live near you, in which case they're a nightmare!)

DOG LOVER/CRAZY CAT PERSON X

This crossbreed is the most dangerous.

They will expect us dogs to share a den with who knows how many cats. Trust me, this is to be avoided at all costs.

Dealing with one cat is bad enough, but if you're outnumbered… it doesn't bear thinking about.

When looking for a human to spend your life with it's important you choose carefully. Check their scent; if there's any whiff of cat, do yourself a favour, pee on their shoe and walk away.

WEAPON

WEAPON

WEAPON

HAIR TRIGGER
ACTIVATES ALL
WEAPONS
INSTANTANEOUSLY

WEAPON

WEAPON

CAT WEAPON SYSTEMS

The above diagram really tells you all you need to know about the anatomy of a cat. Each paw has five razor sharp claws. For those of you that aren't good at math, that adds up to twenty deadly weapons. If you're still struggling to visualise, it's equivalent to a whole box of Bonios. Think about that for a moment, a whole box...

Hello? Yes I'm talking to all you Labradors! Stop thinking about the Bonios now and concentrate back on the job in hand. Honestly you're obsessed!

Not only do cats have sharps in every corner, those tiny mouths are packed with needle teeth. Cats seem to run an all or nothing attack system and the speed in which they change from total relaxation to

17

DEFCON ONE is frankly terrifying.

Oh yeah, they look like butter wouldn't melt in their mouths, they will snuggle up to you, running their little purring engines to indicate that they're happy, pretending to be your friend.

Don't be fooled. They could turn on you at any moment.

If you find yourself in this dubious position, whatever you do don't move, don't blink, don't even look in their direction. Just moving your eyes could disturb the air which may cause a draft.

If even one hair in the trigger area is activated by the resulting breeze, all hell breaks loose.

George found out the hard way...

CAT ATTACK!
MINIMISE THE RISK

Over the years, I have learnt the early warning signs that indicate an imminent cat attack. Look out for these clues:

- Flat ears and spooky black eyes

- Looking at you in a funny way

- The crouch and wiggle manoeuvre - never a good sign, but particularly hazardous if they are peering around a corner or hiding in a bush at the time

- Rolling over and showing their belly. The 'Are you Feeling Lucky Punk' pose. Believe me when I say, this never ends well. Don't fall for it!

- Lastly, don't get taken in by their tails; they speak a completely foreign language! Forget everything you think you know. Waggy tail does not mean happy cat

If you spot any of these signs under no circumstances turn your back on them and DON'T run. Back away very, very slowly.

Don't Try This at Home!

The universal 'meet and greet' rituals that are perfectly acceptable in civilised society, are not appreciated by cats.

Our rather naive comrade Maisy here is about to find out that she has made a serious error of judgement.

We were all puppies once, full of the joys of spring with not a care in the world, thinking life was just one big fun game.

Then cats happen.

We all have to learn the hard way.

These puppies are about to get a chunk of their innocence removed.

FELINE SUPERPOWERS

The ancient Egyptians worshipped cats as gods. Thank goodness humanity has evolved past that nonsense.

Unfortunately, judging by the way they conduct themselves, no one seems to have told cats of this reduction in status.

Where they came from originally, who knows? Perhaps they are not of this earth, which might explain why the laws of gravity don't seem to apply to them.

It's not 'normal' to be able to run up vertical surfaces and just cling there, or jump six times your height from a standing start.

There isn't a building they can't climb, or a roof they can't reach; which is one of their favourite hang-out spots. From there they can sit and look down on all they think they possess.

Cats also have some sort of hyperdrive system that turns them into a blur at top speed. They are fast enough to give Greyhounds a run for their money.

Yes I can hear you Jack Russells... you're very fast as well of course. (How you manage it lugging around those big egos is anyone's guess).

Cats seem impervious to injury. I saw one fall out of a top storey window once. It landed on its feet, paused for a moment looking a bit surprised, then sauntered off as if nothing had happened.

In the same situation a dog would be in need of a stretcher, a visit to the emergency vet and six weeks' cage rest.

Their senses aren't shoddy either. They can see

in the dark, and their hearing is so acute it can pick up a human entering a kitchen from at least a mile away.

By far the most dangerous superpower in the feline arsenal is the ability to twist their entire body around a central point. That middle section is not only a hair trigger for weapons; it's a guidance system as well.

It can swivel and pivot to point weapons in multiple directions all at once, which is both freaky and impossible to deal with.

CAT AMBUSH TECHNIQUES

Cats love sneak attacks.

One of the biggest challenges is the speed they can execute strike and run manoeuvres. By the time the shock and pain register, they have bolted to a position that is invariably out of reach and from there can look at you with utter contempt.

Don't forget to cover your embarrassment by running through your 'shame I can't reach it' routine (more about this later) for the benefit of any witnesses.

It is possible to avoid this indignity. If you can pinpoint where they are lying in wait, you can save yourself a deal of physical pain and mental anguish by giving them a wide berth.

As soon as you get a whiff of cat, be aware and stay vigilant as you run through a thorough reconnaissance:

1. LOOK UP

Most dogs don't have much of a concept of 'up'. (With the exception of squirrel chasers... you know who you are.) This is a particular problem for the ground scenting breeds among us. Cop yourselves on! The enemy are well aware of this flaw and take advantage of it, don't get caught out.

2. CHECK UNDER

Cats could be lurking anywhere. They love to hide under stuff, so search under beds, blankets, bushes and cars.

3. LOOK BEHIND

Check behind corners, curtains, doors, and furniture. Don't forget to look behind the couch which is one of their favourite ambush spots.

Cats aren't always as smart or as sneaky as they like to think they are.

This one obviously isn't very bright:

@ EMAIL FROM FRANK

Dear Bob,
Please help, I'm at my wit's end :(
Last week the humans landed home with this...

I had no idea what it was, but it seemed harmless enough. It was small and furry, had a tail and its eyes were in roughly the right place, the smell though... weird!

But I'd been a bit lonely on my own and I thought, at last a little buddy to play with! I was quite excited.

If only I'd known then, what I know now!

When I tried to introduce myself, something freaky happened! It got HUGE, it must have filled up with air because it started leaking out of its mouth with a loud hiss! Of course I was concerned that it was going to fly away (I've seen balloons do that) so I rushed over to help. That's when this happened...

31

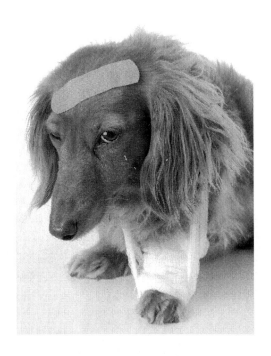

That was the start of the bullying. I can't even use my own bed anymore as 'Twinkles' takes it over and I have to either sleep on the cold floor, or decide which leg is allowed the comfort of the cat's cushion.

The worst is when they leave me alone with it, I can't move without the fear of being attacked.

Please send help!
Yours Desperately,
Frank

@ EMAIL FROM BOB

Dear Frank,

I am so sorry to hear of your cat troubles, those injuries look really painful.

I have attached a free copy of *A Dog's Guide to Cats*. I think you will find it helpful and feel that my Cunning Cat Trap might help you take back control over your life and your bed.

If you don't have the right materials to make one at home, let me have your address, and I'll send one free of charge (See Terms and Conditions).

Drop me an email to let me know how you are getting on.

Thinking about you at this difficult time. Hang in there buddy!

Get well soon,
Woof woof,
Bob.

* Find out how Frank got on later in the book.

WHAT DO CATS DO ALL DAY?

What are cats for and how have they wheedled their way into the lives of our beloved humans?

From what I can ascertain, cats were originally invited into the den for vermin control. I can only assume this trend was started by folk that had been living under a stone and were completely unaware of the existence of terriers.

Being a West Highland terrier myself, I find this rather insulting and not a little hurtful. They don't call us 'Man's Best Friend' for nothing. Only last week I dispatched two rats. You should have seen me, I was magnificent!

Not only do we keep the place clear of vermin, we give companionship, protection, keep them warm, keep them fit, help the blind to see, the deaf to hear, load washing machines for the disabled, we can detect drugs, bombs, cancer and epilepsy. We herd livestock, save lives with search and rescue, put our lives on the line working with the police and armed forces and visit old folks homes, to bring some cheer into the residents lives.

What do cats do?

They kill stuff.

In between killing stuff they seem to do precious little. Just what do cats do all day?

To find out, I decided to go undercover to get photographic evidence of cats going about their daily lives. What I found will shock you.

The first thing that struck me was how much time they spend grooming themselves.

After walks we dogs are pretty good at cleaning off the last of the dirt, but we usually wait until most of it has rubbed off in the car or on the furniture, which is both practical and labour saving. We love playing and rolling around in the muck; the muddier the better, but cats are paranoid about being clean. Where's the fun in that?

VAIN

They waste hours trying to remove imaginary microscopic dust…

There goes a big chunk of their day right there.

At regular intervals during the day, cats stretch their vocal chords to demand food. It's safe to say, their tones aren't dulcet.

Not surprisingly the bipeds give in pretty quick just to shut them up. If they aren't moving quick enough, cats will resort to the leg tangling, purring and rubbing routine that seems to get them what they want.

I have to give grudging admiration to their human training skills, but the frequency and the amount of food they get is taking the p*ss.

GREEDY

If they're not grooming or eating, they are usually lounging about and sleeping. No matter where cats are, they will find the most comfortable places to crash out. Cats are absolutely bone idle, which begs the question, what do they need all that food for?

LAZY

When they're not grooming, eating or sleeping, they are invariably plotting something which normally results in torment for some poor unsuspecting creature.

SCHEMING

How about their work ethic? After weeks of following them around, I finally came across a couple of cats getting on top of the vermin situation.

They have just one job...

USELESS

As vermin control agents, cats are about as useful as a Bonio on a high shelf.

Instead of getting on with the job in hand, they inflict their aggression onto innocent bystanders.

Cats have no concept of emotional attachment and no regard for others feelings.

Imagine the shock when the family came home to find Finny's cold, half-chewed body on the kitchen floor. A fish loved by all who knew him, he died too soon.

Swim in peace under the bridge, golden one.

PETOCIDE MURDERERS

WARNING

The next section is not suitable for puppies.
Parental guidance advised.

FELINE DRUG ADDICTION

During surveillance I discovered a darker and seedier side to feline society.

Some cats have a Catnip problem.

For some individuals, this potent herb is irresistible. The chemical compound in the plant that affects cats is nepetalactone and the attraction to it, is thought to be inherited. So we can also add terrible parenting to the list of feline faults.

Its effects seem to vary depending on how it is taken.

When sniffed, it acts as a stimulant that gives a short and powerful 'high' that makes cats go crazy. (As if they aren't mad enough already!)

It causes dribbling, hallucinations and psychotic episodes that last about ten minutes.

When eaten it has a sedative effect and often leads to a catatonic (pardon the pun) state.

Under the influence of this drug, cats are usually more of a danger to themselves than others.

Good to know.

I'm filing catnip under: 'Things for Future Experimentation and Exploitation'.

WARNING - ADULTS ONLY
Not suitable for Chihuahuas or
anyone else of a nervous disposition

Nothing could have prepared me for what I discovered next. I have long suspected that there was something not right about the fine silkiness of the feline coat.

Turns out it's all fake.

Cats don't have fur at all. You can imagine my horror when I walked in on this naked individual stripped bare of its cuteness cloak.

You can see how this natural look is a more accurate reflection of their warped souls.

It's enough to give you nightmares.

This disturbing revelation made me wonder.

All those different cats that invade my garden, is it just one cat wearing different coats?

Perhaps cats aren't as rampant as they appear to be.

One can only hope.

@ EMAIL FROM JACK

Hi Bob,

I'm not writing this with any hope that you can do anything. I don't think anyone can help me, but I thought if I shared my story it might be good therapy.

This is my bestest friend. His name is Dad and he is the centre of my world.

I take him to the park every day but because he only has two legs, and they are both very old, we like to stop for a while and have a cuddle on our favourite bench so he can have a little rest.

This used to be our 'quality time', just me and Dad... until Tiger decided to tag along. Now as soon as we sit down, the cat takes over Dad's lap.

I'm so upset, it was the only time I got Dad all to myself and I'm missing our cuddles. I think Dad is missing them too, but he is too much of a gentleman to say anything.

Yours with sadness,
Jack

@ EMAIL FROM BOB

Dear Jack,

Don't despair! Me and the lads got together down the park and bounced some ideas around to see if we could come up with a solution.

Woulfe the German Shepherd suggested catnip, he swears by it. Sprinkle some on Tiger's food. While he's chasing rainbows or staring at his naval you and Dad can sneak out without him noticing.

You haven't anything to lose, why not give it a go! I have sourced a supply for you online here:

https://www.amazon.co.uk/KONG-Premium-Catnip-2-oz/dp/B0018N1DRW/

Hoping for a good outcome. Let us know how you get on.

Woof, woof,
Bob

* Will Woulfe's solution work?
Find out later.

PERCEPTIONS: DOGS VS CATS

For the purposes of research, we got together a team of volunteers and sent them out all around the country with a simple survey.

We asked three distinct groups, humans, dogs and cats, one question:

In a fight between a dog and a cat, which do you think would be most likely to win?

The volunteers also asked each group to select a photo that they felt best represented their view of the two species.

The information has been collated, and these are the results:

HUMAN PERCEPTIONS

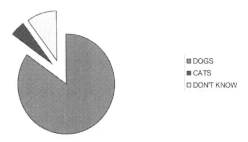

☒ DOGS
■ CATS
☐ DON'T KNOW

A delusional 85% of humanity believe that dogs are 'well able' for cats. A more realistic 5% know just how evil cats are, while 10% of those surveyed didn't have a clue.

When asked to select an image that they felt was a fair representation of dogs and cats, the overwhelming majority chose this image:

CANINE PERCEPTIONS

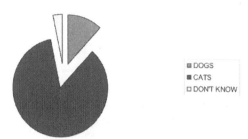

A realistic 85% of dogs know full well that we are in no way 'able' for cats. A delusional 12% (mainly made up of dogs that had never met a cat and Jack Russells who think they're 'hard enough'), thought that dogs would win. While 3% didn't understand the question.

The majority of dogs chose this image:

FELINE PERCEPTIONS

Not surprisingly, 100% of felines had no doubt who would win. (I think I did mention their arrogance previously.)

This view was even held by cats and kittens that had never even heard of, or met a dog.

Their idea of a fair representation of the cat/dog situation:

MAINTAINING THE MYTH

It is unclear how humans came to the conclusion that we are a danger to cats. Perhaps they are harking back to our heritage before *Canis Lupus* gained the *Familiaris* mutation.

Whatever the reason for their misguided views, it's important for the dignity of our species, that we encourage this myth. There are a few methods you can employ to maintain the deception.

The Hold Me Back Manoeuvre

One of the best methods to keep yourself safe, while putting on a really good show of barking, growling and lunging that is bound to impress. This should only be attempted when you have a human on the other end of the lead that is strong enough to prevent you getting anywhere near the cat.

Here you can see Blaze demonstrating the method beautifully.

Out of Reach - What a Shame!

In this situation, it's relatively safe to demonstrate your prowess.

You are letting everyone know - 'If only I could reach that cat, it would be in serious trouble!'

Great for cats on garden fences or up trees.

Windows are our friends

These see-through shields of protection are the best! You can really go to town, safe in the knowledge that there is a physical barrier preventing any actual contact. What a brilliant invention!

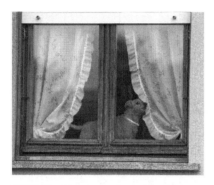

Mobile Dens

Keep a sharp eye open for the enemy whenever you are out in the mobile den. Not only do they have windows, but they move even faster than cats. Humans can't fail to notice our heroics in such a small shared space.

NOTE FROM LOLA

Bless her little heart! Lola has a lot of love to give, no matter what the species.

They are soooo cute sometimz I like to wear one for a hat!

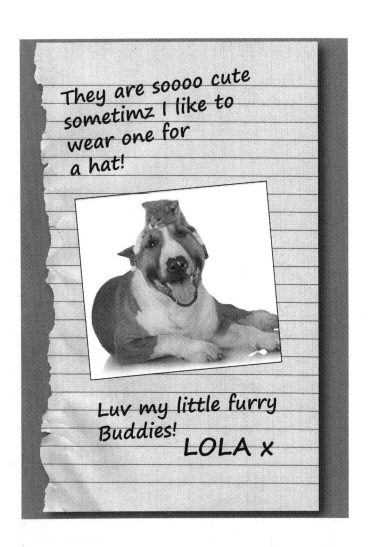

Luv my little furry Buddies! LOLA x

* We will check back with the rather lovely Lola later.

CATS VS DOGS:

INEQUALITY IN THE DEN

What has happened to our once proud species?

Our wolf forefathers must be howling in their graves to see how far we have fallen.

We sacrificed much trading the wild for the couch, and frankly we weren't banking on having to share it with cats.

While our very existence is devoted to pleasing mankind, *they* are only concerned with their own needs.

How is it then, that cats are treated better than us?

What do cats actually contribute to warrant such special treatment?

I commissioned The Institute of Totally Unbiased Canine Studies to conduct scientific research into the value of cats compared to dogs.

59

These are their completely impartial findings:

	Dog	Cat
HOME SECURITY	✓	✗
PERSONAL PROTECTION	✓	✗
COMPANIONSHIP/LOYALTY	✓	✗
EMOTIONAL SUPPORT	✓	✗
NANNY TO KIDS	✓	✗
ASSISTANTS AT WORK	✓	✗
CRAPS IN THE HOUSE	✗	✓
PUKES ON THE BED	✗	✓
KILLS STUFF FOR FUN	✗	✓
PRONE TO SCHIZOPHRENIA	✗	✓

This detailed study proves what I have long suspected - cats are a waste of food.

Food that I could be having.

Food that is considerably better than my food.

Dogs are suffering food poverty, barely surviving on dried out kibble, while cats are served with mouth watering cuisine. Their diet is so superior, their poo is more tasty and nutritious than our dinner.

There is something fundamentally wrong here.

Why, when cats are no good to anybody but themselves, do they get all the best grub?

This was Marmaduke's breakfast...

Marmaduke received this after waking up, stretching, grooming himself and peeing in a box.

And this was my breakfast...

My reward for a nice greeting, a toy offering and fetching of the slippers, which I might add, I had to find first.

Why is this happening? Have cats got some hold over humanity that we are unaware of?

Not only do cats get the best food, every time anyone with opposable thumbs enters the kitchen, they give in to cat demands to be fed. Yet, when I try to do the same thing, I'm told I'm not allowed anything because I'll get *'too fat'*. Fat! Look at me for whining out loud, I'm wasting away!

While I write this, I can hear him at it again.

Hold on... I'm getting a whiff of betrayal. I'll just go and investigate, back in a bit...

Talk about rubbing salt in the wound, this is bordering on dog abuse...

I will not sit back and meekly tolerate this blatant discrimination any longer. It's high time we dogs took action against this violation of basic canine rights. Enough is enough.

CALL TO ARMS

I urge all dogs to stand united on this issue. I have petitioned the government to put in place legislation to ensure hard working dogs are justly compensated for their service to humanity.

As it stands at the moment, we are underappreciated, overworked and underpaid.

I propose an all out strike until our simple and reasonable demands are met.

1) All cats to be banished to the wild. These killing machines do nothing else all day and are quite capable of feeding themselves.

2) After a long day of keeping everyone happy, finding and fetching stuff, walking the bipeds, doing a spot of digging in the garden, dogs should be adequately rewarded for their labours.

Until our demands are met, humans can expect to entertain their own offspring, fetch their own slippers and take themselves to the park.

We are done with being taken for granted!

If you are affected by any of the issues in this article, please contact your local Canine Food Poverty Help Line.

BOB'S CUNNING CAT TRAP

The discovery of our enemy's flaw happened by accident one summer. Luckily I happened to be in the right place at the right time to witness something, that later turned out to be vital intelligence.

It was pantingly hot and I was lounging about in the garden in the shade of my favourite tree, when one of my humans came out of the den with a large box. I was hopeful that it might be full of bones, but alas it was just a paddling pool for the kids. Once it was unpacked, my nose alerted my brain to the scent of cat. I immediately checked the branches above me for aerial attack, and there they were, three of them. But they weren't interested in me, they seemed in a trance-like state mesmerised by the sight of the cardboard box.

Something told me that I had stumbled upon something important, so I wriggled back into the shadows and watched.

Sure enough, at the earliest opportunity they were down the tree, across the garden and into the box. I wondered if there was something special about that particular one, or whether all cardboard containers had the same power.

There was a good supply stacked in the shed, so I decided to run some trials.

Experiment 1: Cat occupation occurred in 2 minutes 30 seconds.

Duration of residence: 3 hours 20 minutes.

I really felt I was on to something. Did the size and shape of the box have an impact?

Experiment 2 Smaller box: Cat occupation in 2 minutes 5 seconds, duration 3 hours 8 minutes.

Experiment 3 Larger box, different location: Two kittens arrived in under 1 minute and stayed for 4 hours 23 minutes.

And so it went on. Each test ended in the successful attraction and containment of cats.

It is unclear why this works as well as it does, but to be honest... who cares? The fact that it does work is all we need to know.

At last we dogs have a system in place that gives us some level of control. For those of you that are unfortunate enough to be landed with the human subspecies Dog Lover/Crazy Cat person X, the multi cat trap is just as easy to set up as the single trap, and should give you hours of cat free pleasure... you're welcome!

If you don't have any boxes lying around the house, you could try some alternatives.

I've had reasonable success with paper bags.

While bags are effective for trapping, they aren't very long lasting and easily shredded by sharp claws. However, they will give some short-term peace.

The cardboard box is by far the best system. You can order one free (while stocks last) Terms and Conditions apply.

Send an email enquiry to:
bobscattrap@cunning.ie

TERMS AND CONDITIONS

All I ask in return is that you make a donation of two Bonios and five Choccy drops to your local dog shelter.

Happy Trapping!

"Twinkles" - Missing August 16

WHERE ARE THEY NOW?

News from Frank:

The bully cat Twinkles, went missing from home some months ago. Knowing that cats have no sense of loyalty whatsoever, I suspect that she probably moved in with some other unsuspecting family.

You can imagine that Frank was ecstatic, but when he noticed how upset his human companions were at Twinkles' disappearance, it made him sad.

He tried everything in his power to cheer them up, but the kids were broken-hearted not knowing what had happened to their cat.

What Frank did next, goes to show you how dedicated, loyal and caring dogs are…

He went out and got them another kitten.

After reading *A Dog's Guide to Cats* Frank felt that he was much better prepared this time and so far, paws crossed, it seems to be working out quite well. The most important thing is that the family are happy.

Fair play Frank, you're a credit to our species.

News from Jack:

Giving Tiger catnip in his food, worked a treat.

While Tiger stays at home chillaxing, Jack and his best friend Dad celebrate getting their quality time back in the park.

Jack couldn't be happier with the outcome.

Well done Woulfe!

(Trust a German to come up with a simple and efficient solution)

The lovely Lola:
Still enjoying her fur babies, the only question she has is which one suits her best, the grey or the striped?

I think she is beautiful, no matter what kitten she is wearing!

I've met up with Lola a few times. Things must be getting serious as she has even introduced me to her little buddies, which I have to admit are very sweet. It's a case of love me, love my cats. I'm hoping that one day in the not too distant future, we might have a family of our own to dote on. Who knows?

And last but not least:

Sir Cecil of Indigo Moon, our friend Diesel, has just moved into his kennel by the sea and is living his dream of a cat free existence.

Due to the generosity of his fellow canines, Diesel was able to buy a state of the art, four room kennel with sun roof.

I couldn't be happier for him, and I'm looking forward to taking up his open invitation to go and visit him for a holiday by the beach.

AND FINALLY

It is my hope that the information contained in *A Dog's Guide to Cats*, has been of help with the daily challenges of life with cats.

If you enjoyed it, please spread the word among your canine friends, we are all in this together. If you can find the time to leave a review, that would be awesome!

Please keep your photos, letters and emails coming. I love hearing about your successes and it helps me gather insightful information that could be of benefit to us all.

If you are worried about something or having problems, tell me about that as well and together, perhaps we can find a solution.

We stand united.

Woof, woof,

Bob

Don't have nightmares…

OTHER PUBLICATIONS

A DOG'S GUIDE TO HUMANS
Written by dogs, for dogs!

Have you ever wondered how dogs see us?

A lighthearted look at the human species from a dog's point of view. Bob the West Highland Terrier shares some tips and tricks on getting the best out of human beings, attempts to fathom some of their strange behaviour and imparts some of his wisdom on training and manipulation techniques.

A must-have book for all canines!

Is YOUR dog a master human trainer?
Take the quiz at the end of the book to find out!

Paperback Edition:-
ISBN-10: 1492841951
ISBN-13: 978-1492841951
Kindle Edition:-
ASIN:B00GF0MJTY

IT SHOULDN'T HAPPEN TO A DOG TRAINER

Have you ever wondered what ends up on the cutting room floor when watching celebrity dog trainers on the television?

During her career as a professional dog trainer and canine behaviourist, Karen Davison has been battered, flattened, tied up in knots and found herself in some funny, strange and painful situations.

Here she shares some of the 'you couldn't make it up' moments that have occurred while working with dogs and their owners

Paperback Edition:-
ISBN-10: 1483906094
ISBN-13: 978-1483906096

Kindle Edition:-
ASIN B00D9PWE02

THE PERFECT COMPANION, Understanding, Training and Bonding with your Dog!

Awarded the IndiePENdents Seal May 2013

This book explores the inner workings of the dog's mind to give you a real understanding of how and why, positive reinforcement gains the best and most reliable results.

You will find detailed instructions on how to teach all the basic commands, using various different positive training techniques, so that you can choose the method that best suits you and your dog.

It encourages you to consider your dog's natural behaviour and to channel their instincts into positive activities, and reveals why stimulating your dog's mind, has many behavioural and physical benefits, possibly contributing to longevity. Environmental enrichment and suggested activities and games, will not only give your dog a confident, happy and fulfilled life, it will also strengthen the bond between you, taking your relationship to a whole new level.

Some common behavioural issues are covered in detail, explaining the causes, prevention and solutions, as well as a general problem solving guide, with a checklist to help you diagnose the root cause of problems, and suggesting what action may be needed, in order to resolve them.

The Perfect Companion, Understanding, Training and Bonding with your Dog! Written by professional dog trainer and canine behaviourist, Karen Davison, is essential reading for all new puppy owners, and a valuable source of information for those of us, who want to get the best out of our relationship with man's best friend

Paperback Edition:-
ISBN-10: 1475235291
ISBN-13: 978-1475235296

Kindle Edition:-
ASIN B0083J6YZ0

COMPLETE GUIDE TO HOUSETRAINING Puppies and Dogs.

Do you need advice on housebreaking your new puppy or older dog?
This guide will give you the means to success!

Take the stress out of housetraining and get positive results - fast. A must have guide for teaching your puppy or dog to be clean in the house. With the right approach, house training can be reasonably quick and easy. This guide shows you how.

Topics covered:- Positive approach, effective clean up regimes, first steps to success, training methods, teaching your dog to go on command, diet and nutrition, advantages and disadvantages of neutering, crate training, common mistakes, dos and don'ts.

Paperback Edition:-
ISBN-10: 1479176893
ISBN-13: 978-1479176892
Kindle Edition:-
ASIN B0090WXMKO

ABOUT THE AUTHOR

Karen Davison grew up in Bedfordshire, England. She has been both an avid reader and a lover of animals since early childhood. When she was eight, the family got their first dog, Scamp, whose great character started Karen's lifelong devotion to dogs.

Since qualifying in Canine Psychology in 2001, she has worked as a professional dog trainer and canine behaviourist. She went on to study Wolf Ecology in 2009 and was lucky enough to spend time with the wolves at the UK Wolf Conservation Trust in Reading.

Her first publication, The Perfect Companion: Understanding, Training and Bonding with your Dog, a comprehensive guide to canine psychology, training and problem solving, was published in June 2012 and won an IndiePENdants award for quality. Since then she has published The Complete Guide to House Training Puppies and Dogs, Companion Huskies: Understanding, Training and Bonding with your Dog, and two Fun Reads for Dog Lovers: It Shouldn't Happen to a Dog Trainer and A Dog's Guide to Humans.

After joining a local writers group, she has spread her author wings and is now enjoying writing poetry, flash fiction and short stories, and after taking a course in screenwriting has just completed her first radio drama script. Karen is also working on her first fiction novel, which combines her love of writing, wolves and fantasy - Wolf Clan Rising which is due to be published 2017.

Karen is now living the dream, she resides in a country cottage on the west coast of Ireland, drawing inspiration for her writing from the peace and beauty of her surroundings where she shares her life with her husband, two daughters and nine special needs pets. Her seven rescue dogs and two rescue cats have a mixture of emotional, behavioural and physical disabilities

One of Karen's favourite sayings: 'Saving one dog will not change the world, but surely for that one dog, the world will change forever'.

Made in the USA
San Bernardino, CA
17 December 2017